Vets Jc

The Ultimate Collection of Jokes for Veterinarians

Published by Glowworm Press
7 Nuffield Way
Abingdon OX14 1RL
By Chester Croker

Jokes for Veterinarians

These jokes for veterinarians will make you giggle. Some of them are old, some of them are current, and while we don't want to plug them too much, we hope you enjoy our collection of the very best veterinarians jokes and puns around.

These jokes about vets will prove you can have a good laugh, and soon with this book you will be laughing out loud.

FOREWORD

When I was asked to write a foreword to this book I was flattered.

That is until I was told that I was the last resort by the author, Chester Croker, and that everyone else he had approached had said they couldn't do it!

I will forgive him though, as I have known Chester for a number of years and his ability to create funny jokes is absolutely incredible. He is quick witted and an expert at crafting clever puns and amusing gags and I feel he is the ideal man to put together a joke book about our profession.

He will be glad you have bought this book, as he has an expensive lifestyle to maintain.

Jack Russell

Table of Contents

Chapter 1: Veterinarian Jokes

If you're looking for funny vets jokes you've certainly come to the right place. These gags were collected by talking to a number of vets, and at the end of this book, you will have the opportunity to upload your joke too, if it's not already in this book.

In this book you will find plenty of cheesy veterinarian jokes that will hopefully make you laugh. Some of them are old, but some of them are new, and we hope you enjoy our collection of the very best vet jokes and puns around.

We've got some great one-liners to start with, plenty of quick fire questions and answers themed gags, some story led jokes and as a bonus some corny pick-up lines for veterinarians.

Chapter 2: One Liner Veterinarian Jokes

Bites, scratches and mysterious stains - 50 shades of veterinary medicine.

Vet to customer "No, we don't actually need anesthesia for dental cleanings. Most pets will just open their mouths and say Ahh."

"I will be honest with you dude, I have a lot of trouble trusting a vet who isn't vegetarian", the dog said to the vet.

Did you hear about the blonde whose computer mouse stopped working? She took it to the vet.

Dog wisdom: - The secret to happiness is never having to wear pants.

If you like being overworked, underappreciated and underpaid become a veterinary technician.

Did you hear about the blonde vet who was learning to tap dance? She kept falling in the sink.

We work in veterinary medicine. You'll have to say a lot to gross us out.

Did you hear about the cross-eyed vet who got sacked because he couldn't see eye to eye with the customers.

Overheard in a vet's surgery:-

"Sorry, I remembered your dog's name and forgot yours."

You know you're a vet tech if you find a hair in your food, pull it out, and keep on eating.

Did you hear about the veterinarian who learned to talk with foxes? She was crazy like a fox.

Overheard in a vet's surgery: - "Cure my dog, but don't touch him, don't do any tests and don't charge me. Oh, did I tell you he bites?"

I got called pretty yesterday and it felt good. Actually, the full sentence was "You're a pretty bad vet." but I'm choosing to focus on the positive.

Did you hear about the junior vet who stole a calendar?

He got twelve months.

You know you're a veterinary technician when you've found toenail clippings in every place imaginable, including your ears, hair, bra, underwear, socks etc. etc.

Murphy's Law of vet med: On the day you have to dress up and go out for dinner, there will inevitably be an IV catheter blood bath, nasal discharge requiring a bath, and ending with a butt flush.

Keep calm and be prepared for National "My dog is having diarrhea" Day.

Top tip to remain safe at a veterinary clinic - don't stand near doors. Those things open fast, and with a vengeance.

Sign seen outside a vet's practise:-

DNA testing done here. Who's your doggie's daddy?

Did you hear about the miracle of the blind vet? He picked up a hammer and saw.

Ever seen a Korean vet? It's not going to happen – they'll eat all their patients.

Of course, I would be more comfortable with you restraining your pet instead of my experienced co-worker doing it.

Did you hear about the work-shy junior vet who used up his sick days, and called in dead.

You might be a vet tech if you think the only way to subdue the drunk hitting on you is with a Rabies pole and an injection of Acepromazine.

My veterinarian colleague told me I should put something away for a rainy day.

I've gone for an umbrella.

A vet wanted to buy something for his dreadful boss, so he bought him a new chair. His boss won't let him plug it in though.

NSFW:- The best thing about being a vet is, I can make a woman show me her pussy then send her husband the bill.

Yesterday, a vet's wife asked him to pass her lipstick but he passed her a super-glue stick instead by mistake. She still isn't talking to him.

Cat puns freak meowt. Seriously – I'm not kitten.

Never trust a dog to watch your food.

Chapter 3: Question and Answer Vet Jokes

Q: What do you get if you cross a dog and a lion?

A: *A terrified veterinarian.*

Q: What did the veterinarian say after the rabbit died?

A: *Hare today, gone tomorrow.*

Q: What did the vet say after she got sued by the cat owner?

A: *You got to be kitten me.*

Q: Why don't veterinarians buy things on Amazon?

A: *They prefer cat-alogues.*

Q: What happens if you cross a chili pepper, a shovel and a terrier?

A: *You get a hot-diggity-dog.*

Q: What do you call a dog magician?

A: *A Labracadabrador.*

Q: What did the sign in the veterinarian's waiting room say?

A: *Be back in 5 minutes. Sit. Stay.*

Q: How to support your local veterinarian?

A: *Buy a Bulldog.*

Q: What's the difference between a rectal and an oral thermometer?

A: *The taste.*

Q: What's the first thing a vet says to a cat?

A: *Hello Kitty.*

Q: What happened when the cat ate a ball of wool?

A: *She had mittens.*

Q: What do you call dental X-Rays?

A: *Tooth pics.*

Q: What do you call a veterinarian who can only treat one species of animal?

A: *A human doctor (MD).*

Q: Why is a tree like a toothless dog?

A: *It's all bark, and no bite.*

Q: What do you call a veterinarian with Laryngitis?

A: *A hoarse doctor.*

Q: What is the only ring a girl doesn't want?

A: *Ring Worm.*

Q: What happened to the Dinosaurs for not going to the vets?

A: *They became extinct.*

Q: How to not get murdered at a veterinary clinic?

A: *Do not comment on the size of veins*

Q: Why did the cat join the Red Cross?

A: *Because it wanted to be a first aid kit.*

Q: What can you do when it rains cats and dogs?

A: *You can step in a poodle.*

Q: What does a pet do after hearing the word "vet"?

A: *It plays dead.*

Q: What did the vet say to the farmer whose cow had no milk?

A: *Sorry, it's an udder failure.*

Q: What do you get if you cross a dog and a lion?

A: *A terrified veterinarian.*

Q: Why can't dalmations hide?

A: *They're always spotted.*

Q: Why do you give a snake Viagra?

A: *Because it has a reptile dysfunction.*

Q: What do you call a vet who is happy every Monday?

A: *Retired.*

Chapter 4: Short Veterinarian Jokes

Our local veterinarian surpassed himself one summer day when a dog was brought to him by a holidaymaker after the dog had an encounter with a porcupine.

After almost an hour of prying, pulling, cutting and stitching, he returned the dog to its owner, who asked what she owed.

"Two hundred and fifty dollars, Madam," he answered.

"That's completely outrageous." she fumed. "That's what's wrong with you Maine people, you're always trying to over-charge summer visitors. Whatever do you do in the winter, when we're not here?"

He cheekily replied "We raise porcupines, Madam."

A vet had a roofer called Gary working on his house repairing some tiles.

Gary is up on the roof and accidentally cuts off his ear, and he yells down to the vet "Hey! Look out for my ear I just cut off!"

The vet looks around and calls up to Gary, "Is this your ear?"

Gary looks down and says "Nope. Mine had a pencil behind it!"

A man takes his poorly dog to the vet.

The vet lifts the dog onto the operating table, looks down and says, "Say ahhh."

The man looks at the vet and says, "The dog can't speak."

The vet looks at the man and says, "I was talking to you. The dog's dead."

Three men met at a party, and it wasn't long until the conversation got around to their line of work and what kind of cars they drove.

"I'm a veterinarian," said the first guy. "So, naturally, I drive a white 'Vet."

As they smiled and nodded, the second man said, "I own a sign company, so I drive a bright blue Neon."

Now the third guy was suddenly quiet until he was egged on by the other two.

"Well," he finally said, "I'm a proctologist, and I have a brown Probe."

At the veterinarian's office, the telephone rings:

A man says "Listen, doctor, tomorrow I'll send my old dog with my wife. Give her a powerful poison so she does not suffer too much."

The vet responds "Okay, but will the dog know how to return home alone?"

A lady took her St Bernard to the vet and said "My dog is cross-eyed, is there anything that you can do for him?"

"Well," said the vet, "let's have a look" and he picks the dog up to have a good look at its eyes. "Hmm, that's not good," says the vet, "I'm going to have to put him down."

The owner was stunned, "Put him down just because he's cross-eyed?"

"No," replies the vet "because he's very heavy."

A vet is struggling to find a parking space.

"Lord," he prayed. "I can't stand this. If you open a space up for me, I swear I'll give up the booze and go to church every Sunday."

Suddenly, the clouds part and the sun shines on an empty parking spot.

Without hesitation, the vet says: "Never mind Lord, I found one."

A vet tries to enter a bar wearing a shirt open at the collar, and is met by a bouncer who tells him that he must wear a necktie to gain admission.

So the vet goes to his car to try and find a necktie but he can't find one.

However he knows he has some jump leads in his boot; and in desperation he ties these around his neck, and manages to fashion a knot and lets the cable ends dangle free.

He goes back to the bar and the bouncer carefully looks him over, and then says: "I guess you can come in now, but just don't start anything."

A veterinarian in my area went to jail for dealing drugs.

I've been one of his customers for well over five years, and I had no idea he was a vet.

A scruffy dog walks into a pub, and takes a seat. He says to the barman, "Can I have a pint of beer please."

The barman says, "Wow, that's incredible; you should join the circus."

The scruffy dog replies, "Why? Are they looking for vets?"

A veterinarian was feeling ill and went to see her doctor.

The doctor asked her all the usual questions, about symptoms, how long had they been occurring, etc., when she interrupted him, saying, "Hey look, I'm a vet. I don't need to ask my patients these kinds of questions. I can tell what's wrong just by looking. Why can't you?"

The doctor nodded, looked her up and down, wrote out a prescription, and handed it to her and said, "There you are. Of course, if that doesn't work, we'll have to have you put down."

A guy brings his dog into the vet and says, "Could you please cut my dog's tail off?"

The vet examines the tail and says, "There is nothing wrong. Why would you want this done?"

The man replies, "My mother-in-law is coming to visit, and I don't want anything in the house to make her think that she is welcome."

I was taking my dog out the other day when I met this bloke who asked me where I was going.

The dog was foaming at the mouth, so I explained that I was on my way to the vet to have him put down.

The bloke asked me, "Is he mad?" to which I replied, "Well, he's not exactly pleased about it."

A vet goes to the doctor with a hearing problem.

The doctor says, "Can you describe the symptoms to me?"

The vet replies "Yes. Homer is a fat yellow lazy man and his wife Marge is skinny with big blue hair."

A vet meets up with his blonde girlfriend as she's picking up her car from the auto repairers.

"Everything ok with your car now?" he asks.

"Yes, thank goodness," the dipsy blonde replies.

The vet asks, "Weren't you worried the mechanic might try to rip you off?"

The dozy blonde replies, "Yes, but he didn't. I was so relieved when he told me that all I needed was blinker fluid!"

The homeowner was delighted with the way the vet had looked after his Tibetan Masstif.

"You did a great job." he said and paid his bill. "Also, in order to thank-you, here's an extra 50 bucks to take the missus out to dinner."

Later that night, the doorbell rang and it was the vet. The homeowner asked him, "Did you forget something?"

"Nope." replied the vet, "I'm just here to take your missus out to dinner like you asked."

A vet came to my house to check up on my Irish Setter, and they ran around the garden together.

I had just finished washing the floor when the vet asked to use the toilet.

With dismay I looked at his muddy boots and my newly polished floor. "Just a minute," I said, "I'll put down some newspaper."

"That's all right, madam" he responded. "I'm house trained."

An old vet was walking along the road one day when he came across a frog.

He reached down, picked the frog up, and started to put it in his pocket. As he did so, the frog said, "Kiss me on the lips and I'll turn into a beautiful woman."

The old vet carried on putting the frog in his pocket.

The frog said, "Didn't you hear what I said?"

The vet looked at the frog and said, "Yes, but at my age I'd rather have a talking frog."

One day at the veterinarian's office where I take my cat, a man and the receptionist were verbally sparring.

After a few moments a technician came to her co-worker's defense saying "Sir, do you know what happens to aggressive males in this office?"

Here are some gags for the kids:-

Boy: "I have a dog that doesn't have a nose."

Vet: "How does he smell?"

Boy: "Awful."

The vet asks the pony, "Have you a sore throat?

"No", says the pony, "I'm just feeling a little hoarse."

Next patient is a puppy. The vet asks, "How are you feeling?" and the puppy answers, "Rough."

Chapter 5: Longer Veterinarian Jokes

A woman walks into a veterinarian's waiting room dragging a wet rabbit on a leash. The rabbit obviously does not want to be there.

"Sit down Thumper." she says. Thumper glares at her, and sopping wet, jumps up on another customer's lap, dripping water on them.

"I said sit, now there's a good rabbit," says the embarrassed woman.

Thumper, wet already, squats in the middle of the room and urinates. The woman then yells, - "Thumper, will you please be good?"

Thumper then starts a fight with a bulldog and they both run out of the surgery.

As the woman leaves to chase after Thumper, she turns to the other customers and says: "You will have to excuse me; I just washed my hare, and I can't do a thing with it."

There was a country doctor who was the only doctor for miles around.

He wanted to go on a fishing trip, so he called the vet and asked him to look after things while he was gone.

The vet asked, "Is anything happening?"

The doctor replied, "Mrs. Jones is about due, but I don't think the baby will come before I get back. Anyway, if it does, just deliver it. This is her third, and the first two went really easily."

The vet agreed, and the doctor went on the fishing trip.

When he returned, he called the vet and asked, "How did things go while I was gone?"

The vet replied, "Pretty good. Mrs. Jones had her baby. It was an eight pound boy. Everyone's doing fine."

The doctor asked, "Did you have any trouble?"

The vet replied, "Well, there was just one little problem. I had a terrible time getting her to eat the afterbirth."

My wife found out that our dog (a Giant Schnauzer) could hardly hear, so she took it to the vets and he told her that the problem was hair in the dog's ears.

He cleaned both ears, and the dog could then hear fine. The vet then proceeded to tell my wife that, to fix it for good, she should get some special hair remover and rub it in the dog's ears once a week.

So she went to the store and bought this special hair remover.

The pharmacist told her, "If you're going to use this under your arms, don't use deodorant for a few days."

She said, "I'm not using it under my arms."

The pharmacist said, "If you're using it on your legs, then don't use body lotion for a couple of days."

She replied, "I'm not using it on my legs either. If you must know, I'm going to use it on my Giant Schnauzer."

The pharmacist said, "Well, then stay off your bicycle for at least a week."

One hot July day we found an old straggly cat at our door.

She was a sorry sight. Starving, dirty, smelled terrible, skinny and hair all matted down. We felt sorry for the cat so we put her in a carrier and took her to the vet.

She had no name so we named her Pussy cat. The vet decided to keep her for a day or so and said he would let us know when we could come and get her.

My husband said, "OK, but don't forget to wash her, she stinks."

Next day my husband had an appointment with his doctor, which was located next door to the vet.

The doctor's office was full of people waiting to see the doctor. In the midst of the waiting room crowd, a side door opened and in leaned the vet; and he had obviously seen my husband arrive.

He looked straight at my husband and said, "Your wife's pussy is finally clean and shaved. She now smells like a rose. And by the way, I think she's pregnant. God knows who the father is." He then closed the door.

Ron is with two of his friends, Jim and Shamus.

Jim says, "I think my wife is having an affair with a vet. The other day I came home and found some nail trimmers under our bed and they're not mine."

Shamus then confides, "Wow, me too! I think my wife is having an affair with an electrician. The other day I found some wire cutters under the bed and they aren't mine."

Ron thinks for a minute and then says, "You know - I think my wife is having an affair with a horse."

Both Jim and Shamus look at him in disbelief.

Ron sees them looking at him and says, "No, seriously. The other day I came home early and found a jockey under our bed."

A veterinarian surgeon had had a long tiring day, but when he got home from tending to all the sick animals his wife was waiting with a cold beer and a delicious meal, after which they had a few more drinks and went to bed.

At 3:30 in the morning, the phone rang.

"Is that the vet?" asked an elderly woman's voice.

"Yes, it is", replied the vet, "Is this an emergency?"

"Well, I think so", said the elderly lady, "there's a whole loads of cats on next door's roof making a terrible din and I can't get to sleep. What should I do about it?"

There was a big sigh from the vet, who then replied "Open the window and tell them they're needed on the phone."

The elderly lady replied, "Will that stop them?"

"It should do," said the vet, "It stopped me."

A vet is called to the house of a delicate old woman to check up on her Doberman. The dog is drooling and growling under his breath and he has a parrot whistling contentedly next to him on his perch.

After five minutes, the little old lady excuses herself. The vet asks the little old lady if he'll be safe while she's away to which she smiles and says: "Oh yes. Poopsie is so sweet. But whatever you do, do NOT say anything to the parrot!"

Relieved, the vet tries to continue his examination. However, the parrot starts making a horrible racket and is calling the vet some dreadful rude names.

The vet cannot concentrate on his work. Losing his temper, the vet glares at the parrot and shouts: "Will you be quiet, you useless bird", and he goes back to assessing the dog.

The bird is stunned into complete silence. Just ten seconds later, the parrot squawks: "Stick it to him, Poopsie!"

A farmer went to his local bank to borrow money for a new bull. The loan was made and the banker came by a week later to see how the bull was doing.

The farmer complained that the bull just ate grass and wouldn't even look at a cow.

The banker suggested that he have a veterinarian take a look at the bull.

Next week, the banker returned to see if the vet had helped.

The farmer looked very pleased. "The bull has serviced all of my cows! He broke through the fence, and bred all my neighbor's cows! He's been breeding just about everything in sight. He's like a machine!"

"Wow," said the banker, "what did the vet do to the bull?"

"Just gave him some pills," replied the farmer.

"What kind of pills?" asked the banker.

"I don't know," replied the farmer "but they kind of taste like peppermint."

A guy sees an old man in town at a coffee shop bawling his eyes out, and he asks him what the problem is.

"I've had a great life," says the old man. "I was a successful vet, and I sold my vet surgery for a large amount of money."

The guy says, "So what's the problem then?"

The old man says, "I own a large house complete with a pool."

The guy looks puzzled and says, "So what is the problem?"

The old man cries saying, "I own two fast cars."

The guy looks confused and says, "I'm with you so far, but I still don't see what the problem is."

The old man simply says, "Just last month I got married to an ex Penthouse Pet."

The guy scratches his head and says, "What exactly is the problem?"

The old man sobs, "I can't remember where I live!"

A man walks into the vets with his pet budgie saying it is ill.

The vet says "Sorry, there is nothing that I can do for him."

The man is not happy and he asks for a second opinion.

The vet then walks out and his partner comes in with a cat; the cat looks at the budgie and shakes his head; the vet then brings in a labrador and the dog looks at the budgie and also shakes his head.

The second vet says, "I'm sorry there is nothing we can do for him"

As the man leaves the vets give him a bill for 400 dollars and the man asks "Why is the bill so high?"

The vet replies, "Well, you had 2 opinions, then a cat scan and also a lab report."

Carlo the property developer and his vet buddy Doug, went bar-hopping every week together after golf, and every week Carlo would go home with a different woman while Doug went home alone.

One week Doug asked Carlo his secret to picking up women.

"Well, it's easy," said Carlo "When you're out on the dance floor and she asks you what you do for a living, don't tell her you're a vet. Tell her you're a lawyer instead."

Later Doug is dancing with a woman when she leans in and asks him what he does for a living.

"I'm a lawyer," says Doug.

The woman smiles seductively and says, "Want to go back to my place? It's just around the corner."

They go to her place, have some fun and an hour later, Doug is back in the pub telling Carlo about his success.

"I've only been a lawyer for an hour," Doug snickered, "And I've already screwed someone!"

A vet, a lawyer, a beautiful lady, and an old woman were on a train, sitting 2x2 facing each other.

The train went into a tunnel and when the carriage went completely dark, a loud "smack" was heard.

When the train came out of the tunnel back into the light the lawyer had a red hand print on his face. He had been slapped on the face.

The old lady thought, "That lawyer must have groped the young lady in the dark and she slapped him."

The hottie thought, "That lawyer must have tried to grope me, got the old lady by mistake, and she slapped him."

The lawyer thought, "That vet must have groped the hottie, she thought it was me, and slapped me."

The vet just sat there thinking, "I can't wait for another tunnel so I can slap that lawyer again!"

Take your pick from the next two gags:-

The female vet complained to her friend that her husband didn't satisfy her anymore.

Her friend recommended she find another man on the side.

When they met up a month or so later, the vet told her friend "I took your advice. I managed to find a man on the side, yet my husband still doesn't satisfy me!"

The male vet complained to his friend that his wife didn't satisfy him anymore.

His friend recommended he find another woman on the side.

When they met up a month or so later, the vet told his friend "I took your advice. I managed to find a woman on the side, yet my wife still doesn't satisfy me!"

A young vet is sitting at a bar one night, when a large sweaty construction worker sits next to her.

They start talking and ultimately the conversation gets on to nuclear war.

The vet asks the construction worker, "If you hear the sirens go off, the missiles are on their way, and you've only got 20 minutes left to live, just what would you do?"

The construction worker replies, "I'm going to get it together with anything that moves."

The construction worker then asks the vet what she would do to which she replies, "I'm going to keep perfectly still."

A male vet was talking to two of his friends about their daughters.

His first friend says "I was cleaning my daughter's room the other day and I found a pack of cigarettes. I didn't even know she smoked."

His second friend says, "That's nothing. I was cleaning my daughter's room the other day and I found a half full bottle of red wine. I didn't even know she drank."

The vet then says, "That's nothing. I was cleaning my daughter's room the other day and I found a pack of condoms. I didn't even know she had a penis."

A group of vets, all aged 40, discussed where they should meet for a reunion lunch. They agreed to meet at a place called The Red Lion because the atmosphere was lively and the staff were fun.

Ten years later, at age 50, the vets once again discussed where they should meet for lunch.

It was agreed they would meet at The Red Lion because the food and service was good and there was an excellent beer selection.

Ten years later, at age 60, the friends again discussed where they should meet for lunch.

It was agreed they would meet at The Red Lion because there were plenty of parking spaces, they could dine in peace and quiet, and it was good value for money.

Ten years later, at age 70, the friends discussed where they should meet for lunch.

It was agreed they would meet at The Red Lion because the restaurant was wheelchair accessible and had a toilet for the disabled.

Ten years later, at age 80, the vets, now all retired, discussed where they should meet for lunch.

Finally it was agreed they would meet at The Red Lion because they had never been there before.

A woman has a poorly cat, which is suffering from constipation, so she takes it to the vet, who gives her a new kind of laxative.

The vet tells her, "Give her about four teaspoons of this, and she'll be better in no time."

The woman does as she's told and returns a week later.

The vet asks, "How's your calf?"

The woman replies, "I don't have a calf. It was my cat who wasn't feeling well."

The vet asks, "Well, how's your cat doing?"

The woman replies, "I'm not sure. The last time I saw her, she was heading toward the north end of town with ten other cats. Five were digging, three were covering, and two were scouting for new territory."

A guy took his bulldog along to the vets after getting several complaints from the mailman.

The vet said, "I don't see anything wrong with your dog other than the fact that he is old, and through my years of practice, I recommend you castrating him so he will mellow out a bit."

The guy agreed, and after his bulldog had recovered from the operation, his owner let him out onto the porch again.

Along came the mailman, and up jumped the dog, knocked the mailman down and bit his ass.

The dog's owner apologized to the mailman, saying he had got the dog castrated and he was acting strangely.

The mailman brushed himself off and said, "That was a mistake; he didn't want to hump me. You should have had his teeth pulled out instead."

A father and his son are driving to the vet's office with their prize lamb. They get to the office and the vet askes, "what seems to be the problem with fine animal?"

The father answers, "Well, he just seems to be acting strange around every time we go out to the barn to see him."

The little boy begins to sob, "Doctor, can you please help my poor sheep? We have been through so much together; I have raised him since he was only a few days old."

The vet reassures the boy, "Don't worry son, I have a machine in the back and if I put your sheep on it he will be able to tell me everything that has been going on with him."

The vet leaves the room with the sheep, and the boy sits quietly staring at the floor.

He then looks at his father and says, "I think that we should leave now. I know that sheep and I know as soon as it's the two of them back there, he's going to tell the vet all kinds of lies about me."

Chapter 6: Veterinarian Pick Up Lines

I've got a thermometer and a jar of Vaseline with your name on it, fuzzy butt.

I've been bad. Wanna rub my nose in it and spank me?

I think I'm going to have to put you down tonight.

Whoa. Look at those puppies.

Your beak says no, but your tail feathers say yes.

If I look at you any longer, I'll have to put on a satellite dish collar to keep from licking myself raw."

Can I do it doggie style?

If I said you had a beautiful body, would you hump my leg?

Give me a kiss. Give me a kiss. Who's a good girl? Yes, you are a very good girl.

Has this bar stool already been marked?

Is it warm in here, or are you in heat?

Oooh, your butt smells great -- is that Obsession?

But that's 21 in dog inches.

Baby, I feel a hose-spraying in our immediate future.

Chapter 7: Bumper Stickers for Veterinarians

Veterinary Medicine: Because humans are gross.

Vet techs are pawsome.

Real doctors (Vets) treat more than one species.

I am a vet tech. Hear me roar.

Don't argue with your veterinarian. They know how to neuter.

Veterinary technicians: Always surrounded by their best friends.

About the Author

Chester Croker, known to his friends as Chester The Jester, has written many joke books and has twice been named Comedy Writer Of The Year by the International Jokers Guild. He has owned a number of pets over the years and has always been appreciative of the great work that vets do. When he was asked to write this vets joke book, he simply jumped at the chance.

I hope you enjoyed this book and if you did, could you please leave a review on Amazon so that other vets can have a good laugh too.

If you see anything wrong, or you have a gag you would like to see included in the next version of this book, please visit the glowwormpress.com website.

Final note:

Saving the life of one animal may not change the world, but it will change the world for one animal.